To Wini
with love
Mary

September 1988

Under the Snowball Tree
Written and Illustrated by Ellie Kirby

Copyright 1986
Fox Creek Press
Route 2, Box 250
Troutdale, Virginia 24378

Under the Snowball Tree

Dedicated to Ba

Who Read to Me

SOMEWHERE over the mountains
In a meadow where cows wander
And apple trees bloom in the spring
There is a house

A big white house
With morning glories all around the porch
And a yard full of ducks and chickens
Who wake up early to announce
It's time to rise and shine

Anna gets up first
She settles into the big red chair
To read the day's news
The morning says hello

Suzie sits with her girls on the back porch
She combs out the tangles of the night
And puts Mae's hair into two braids
Long and black and fine

Anna and Mae blow bubbles
Lovely and fragile as our dreams
They float
Light as any wish
They drift
Reflecting the world as they turn

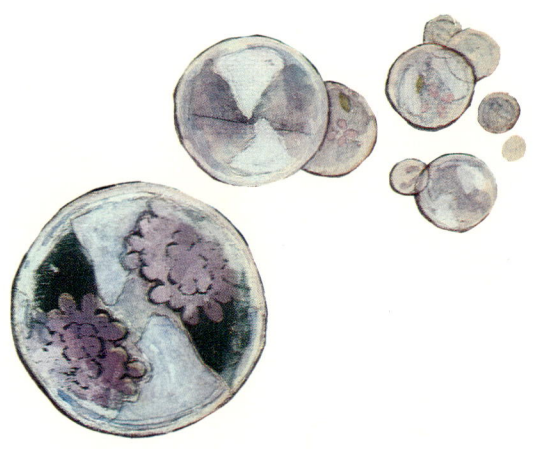

Suzie washes some clothes
And hangs them on the line
To catch the wind and soak in the sun
Warm and crisp and dry
They smell of sweet breezes

In Suzie's garden the sunflowers chat
And look to see how the garden is growing
Cabbages squat
And think their little thoughts
Beans twine and stretch to the sun
Curling their tendrils in delight

Mae climbs the ladder
Up into her treehouse
The branches of the snowball tree
Lift and hold her
Out of everyone's reach

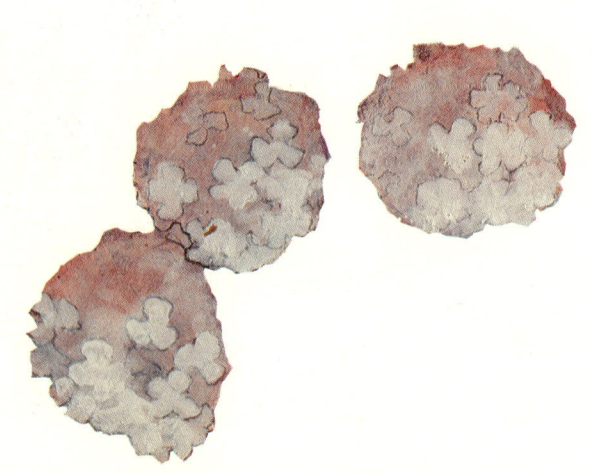

Suzie's friends come over to play music
Under the snowball tree they play and play
Tunes catch the breeze
And drift out over the fields
To tickle the ears of wandering cows

After supper it's time to do dishes
First scrub them in the warm soapy water
Then towel dry to a sheen
(Can you see yourself?)
Now put them gently up to rest in their cupboard.

Suzie reads a story to Mae
The story grows and grows
Until it fills the whole room
And even the snowball tree
Leans at the window to listen

And now to bed
To slip between the sheets
And curl up under the covers and stars
Into a little sleep

And to drift out
To where cows at their leisure
Wander into the house
Through the dark halls
Up the chimney
And out onto the roof
They ask important questions
(Who can remember the reply?)

But the house dreams on
Into the night
Holding, cradling all within
Tight and warm in the darkness
Goodnight
Goodnight.